THE LITTLE GUIDE TO

HERMÈS

First published in 2025 by OH
An Imprint of HEADLINE PUBLISHING GROUP LIMITED

1

Disclaimer:

This book has not been licensed, approved, sponsored, or endorsed by Hermès or any rightsholder(s) in respect of this brand.

Hermès is a registered trademark owned by Hermès International

Cataloguing in Publication Data is available from the British Library

ISBN 978-1-03542-260-9

Compiled and written by: Katie Meegan
Editorial: Saneaah Muhammad
Designed and typeset in Avenir by: Stephen Cary
Project manager: Russell Porter
Production: Arlene Lestrade
Printed and bound in China

Headline's policy is to use papers that are natural, renewable and recyclable products and made from wood grown in well-managed forests and other controlled sources. The logging and manufacturing processes are expected to conform to the environmental regulations of the country of origin.

HEADLINE PUBLISHING GROUP LIMITED
An Hachette UK Company
Carmelite House, 50 Victoria Embankment, London EC4Y 0DZ

The authorised representative in the EEA is Hachette Ireland, 8 Castlecourt Centre, Dublin 15, D15 XTP3, Ireland (email: info@hbgi.ie)

www.headline.co.uk   www.hachette.co.uk

THE LITTLE GUIDE TO

HERMÈS

STYLE TO LIVE BY

Unofficial and Unauthorized

CONTENTS

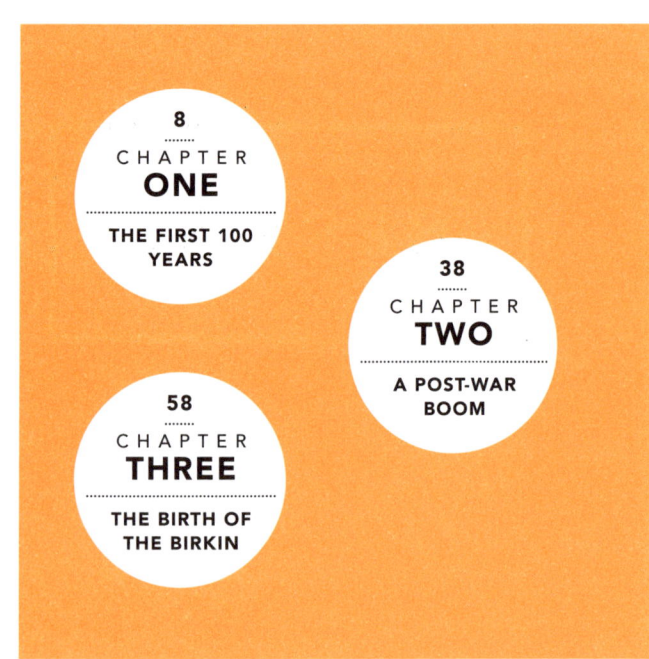

INTRODUCTION

There are few fashion houses quite like Hermès. The legacy, the prestige and the devotion to craft are as prominent today as they were when it was founded by Theirry Hermès in 1837. What began as a maker of finely crafted saddles and harnesses for the aristocracy has evolved into a global symbol of craftsmanship, elegance and enduring style. Now run by the sixth generation of the Hermès-Dumas dynasty, the fashion house is today synonymous with quality and exclusivity.

The story of Hermès begins with Thierry Hermès, a skilled harness maker who opened his workshop in Paris to cater to the needs of horse-drawn carriage owners in the 19th century. In 1922, his grandson Émile-Maurice Hermès took over the business, expanding its horizons into leather goods, fashion and accessories. Under his leadership, the company's signature craftsmanship was introduced to new fields, and Hermès quickly became known for its luxury leather handbags, silk scarves and refined ready-to-wear collections.

The Hermès family has remained at the helm of the company for several generations, nurturing its growth and ensuring its commitment to tradition and innovation. From the introduction of the zipper into clothing, using the fastening on motor cars as inspiration, or the creation of the first bags, right down to the appointment of Jean Paul Gaultier to womenswear or the collaboration with the Apple watch, Hermès continues to seamlessly combine the classic and traditional with the groundbreaking and unexpected.

With some of the most iconic collections in the history of fashion, from Birkin and Kelly bags to revolutionary silk printed carré scarves, and inspired by everything from equestrian motifs to fantastical creatures, each design created by Hermès demonstrates the brand's continued commitment to quality.

This little guide takes you through the history, key collections and values that have made Hermès a global icon, a patron of the arts and the symbol of timeless luxury that it is today.

CHAPTER
ONE

THE FIRST
100 YEARS

FROM ITS FOUNDING IN 1837,
HERMÈS HAS REMAINED ONE OF
THE FEW FASHION HOUSES, NAY
BUSINESSES, TO STILL BE RUN BY
ITS FOUNDER'S DESCENDANTS
NEARLY TWO CENTURIES LATER.

THIS BLEND OF TRADITIONALISM
AND ITS EMBRACE OF FRESH IDEAS
WITH EACH NEW GENERATION
MAKES HERMÈS A TRULY UNIQUE
ENTERPRISE.

The story of Hermès begins over 220 years ago with the birth of Thierry Hermès in 1801.

The sixth child of a French mother and a German father, Thierry was raised in Krefeld, Germany, which was a part of Napoleon's First Republic at the time.

Renowned for its textiles industry, Krefeld was also known as *Stadt wie samt und seide*, or "the city of velvet and silk".

The world is divided into two:
those who know how to use tools,
and those who do not.

Jean-Louis Dumas

Former Hermès CEO and Thierry Hermès' great-great-great-
grandson, vanityfair.com, August 27, 2007

After losing his entire family to disease and war, Thierry moved to France in 1821 as an orphan.

Gifted in leatherworking, he opened a saddle and harness shop in the Parisian neighbourhood of Grands Boulevards in 1837.

The freedom to create, the constant quest for beautiful materials, and the transmission of exceptional know-how – which enable the creation of useful and elegant objects, which stand the test of time – forge the uniqueness of Hermès.

Hermès

hermes.com, 2024

Thanks to a specialized saddle stitching technique, Hermès quickly built a reputation among France's fashionable elite.

Some of his most notable clients of the time included European royalty, as well as Emperor Napoleon III!

Upon his father's death in 1880, Charles-Émile Hermès took over the business and moved the atelier to 24 rue du Faubourg Saint-Honoré, Paris, where it remains to this day.

Few brands will ever reach the iconic status, exquisite quality and elegance achieved by the French luxury fashion house Hermès. With its emphasis on functionality, beauty, quality and artisan craftsmanship, it has surpassed the test of time.

Laia Farran Graves

The Story of the Hermès Scarf, Laia Farran Graves, 2023

Heads of Hermès: A timeline

Theirry Hermès
1837–1878

Charles-Émile Hermès
1878–1902

Adolphe and Émile-Maurice
(Hermès Frères) *1902–1919*

Émile Hermès
1919–1951

Robert Dumas-Hermès
1951–1978

Jean-Louis Dumas
1978–2006

**Pierre-Alexis Dumas
(artistic director)**
2005–present

Patrick Thomas
2006–2012

Axel Dumas
2012–present

Charles-Émile Hermès steadily steered the saddlery until he was succeeded by his sons Adolphe and Émile-Maurice (often referred to simply as Émile).

The pair renamed the company Hermès Frères, and by 1914, they had employed up to eighty saddle craftsmen. Their esteemed clientele included the last tsar of Russia, Nikolai II.

Many years ago, before my time, Mr Émile Hermès frequently travelled to different countries. He left with a trunk made of leather, obviously, and filled it with miniature models of Hermès tack to present to potential customers. On his return, the craftsmen worked flat out for months on end to keep up with the new orders.

Raymonde Ottaway

Former Hermès artisan, recalling an anecdote that her father-in-law, a second-generation Hermès saddler, shared, *Hermès: Straight from the Horse's Mouth*, Luc Charbain, 2022

"

[Hermès] is an old company with a Protestant spine and a Parisian perfectionism, one of the oldest family-owned-and-controlled companies in France.

"

Laura Jacobs

Vanity Fair Editor on the unique DNA that Hermès possesses, vanityfair.com, August 27, 2007

During the interwar period, demand for saddlery decreased in tandem with the rise of the motor car.

Now the sole manager, Émile expanded Hermès' offerings to include leather goods, bags and accessories.

His golden rule was beauty through usefulness.

Ménéhould de Bazelaire du Chatelle

Director of Cultural Heritage, Hermès, on Émile Hermès, classicchicagomagazine.com, 2024

Leather, sport and a tradition
of refined elegance.

Émile Hermès

On the philosophy of the brand during his tenure, *Contemporary Fashion*, Richard Martin, 1995

My grandfather, during the war, was sent as an officer to the States, and he met [Henry] Ford. At that time it was the best example for factories in the world. And in Canada he found a kind of zip, for the [canvas] roof of the cars. He thought it was something he could use in France – to make other things.

Jérôme Guerrand

Chairman of the Hermès supervisory board, on his grandfather's creation of the garment zip, vanityfair.com, August 27, 2007

Upon a trip to Canada, Émile Hermès was fascinated by the zipping system used on the hoods of military cars. In 1922, he obtained exclusive rights to this "closing system" in France.

Due to these exclusive rights, the zipper in France was known as the *fermeture Hermès* (Hermès fastener).

Every time an artist, a designer for Hermès, comes here, they are excited. They feel energy from the craftsmanship.

Ménéhould de Bazelaire

Curator of the Hermès museum, on the intersection of history and innovation found in the Hermès archives, vanityfair.com, August 27, 2007

It was in 1922 that Hermès also began to pour effort into creating handbags.

Émile Hermès' wife complained that she couldn't find a practical and stylish bag that she liked, prompting her husband to create a smaller version of the Haut à Courroies saddlebag.

Haut à Courroies

Translating to "high-belt" in French, the name is a reference to the straps that latch around the top of the bag.

It was the first bag produced by Hermès.

Sturdy and elegant, the bag was originally designed for horse riders who needed an elevated way to carry their saddles and boots.

Full of character, the format is ideal for those who like to ride through life and over its obstacles with elegance.

Hermès

Describing the modern remake of the Haut à Courroies bag, hermes.com, 2024

The Haut à Courroies handbag was a success, and in 1925, Hermès released a range of travel bags.

After launching in America, in the department store Neiman Marcus, they were a hit with the new breed of globe-trotting elite.

I think Hermès objects are desirable because they reconnect people to their humanity… Our customer feels the presence of the person who crafted the object, while at the same time the object brings him back to his own sensitivity, because it gives him pleasure through his senses.

Pierre-Alexis Dumas

Former CEO and Hermès descendant on the uniqueness of the Hermès model, businessinsider.com, February 24, 2024

We will continue to make things the way the grandfathers of our grandfathers did.

Jean-Louis Dumas

Late Hermès CEO on continuing family traditions, vanityfair.com, August 27, 2007

The Hermès Saddle Stitch

Devised by founder Thierry Hermès and still in use today, this is a two-needle process creating remarkably strong seams.

Far from the equestrian equipment it was devised for, the saddle stitch is now used on every Hermès bag.

"

It's not really about the stitch.
It's about being aware of the sense
of touch, being able to stitch with
your eyes closed, being able to
represent yourself and the object
you're making in space, being
able to listen to what your hands
tell you.

"

Pierre-Alexis

Artistic co-director and Hermès descendant on learning the saddle
stitch from the age of 10, vanityfair.com, August 27, 2007

Throughout the 1920s and 1930s, Hermès expanded into the United States and resort towns of France.

It is during this period that many of the most recognizable pieces were introduced, including handbags, scarves and the riding jacket.

CHAPTER
TWO

A POST-WAR BOOM

WHILE WESTERN EUROPE
STRUGGLED IN POST-WORLD-WAR-
TWO RECESSION AND RECOVERY,
THE HOUSE OF HERMÈS WAS
QUIETLY MAKING WAVES WITH
STEADY DEDICATION TO THE
CRAFT OF LEATHERWORKING AND
ELEVATED FINERY.

"

It has been said of Hermès, that
it is perhaps the only establishment
in the world in which one cannot
buy a single article that is not in
perfect taste.

"

The New York Times, May 13, 1940

Émile fathered four daughters, one of whom died young. In order to keep the business in the family, Émile groomed his sons-in-law to eventually take over.

After years working together, Robert Dumas (he would also adapt the name Hermès) succeeded Émile after his death in 1951. For the first time in its history, Hermès was passed to a son-in-law.

66

I asked [Robert Dumas], 'what is it about Hermès? If you can say one thing, what is it?' And he said to me, 'Hermès is different because we are making a product that we can repair.' It's so simple. And it's not so simple.

99

Pascale Mussard

Hermès descendant and co-artistic director of Hermès reflecting on a conversation she had with Robert Dumas-Hermès, vanityfair.com, August 27, 2007

The famous orange Hermès packaging was accidental in origin.

Due to World War Two in 1942, the usual cream packaging that the luxury goods house preferred was hard to come by, so Robert Dumas-Hermès had to accept the only colour left: orange!

Whether round, rectangular or square, it is used to package ties, hats, boots, tableware, jewellery or bags. Only furniture is too large to fit inside one… Attractive and robust, its qualities make it an iconic object in its own right.

Hermès

Describing the Hermès orange box, hermes.com, 2024

Did you know that the Hermès box is so iconic that it actually won an Oscar in 1994 (the prestigious packaging award)?

In 1935, Hermès launched the Sac à Dépêches bag, inspired, much like the Haut à Courroies bag, by timeless elegant utility.

Kelly bags are the epitome
of refinement.

Karen Homer

The Little Book of Hermès, Karen Homer, 2022

In 1956, the American actress-turned-royal and long-time client of Hermès, Grace Kelly, was continuously followed by paparazzi.

Not wanting to reveal the early stages of her pregnancy, she hid her stomach behind an Hermès Sac à Dépêches bag.

Famous worldwide, the now iconic photographs led to the public to nicknaming the bag, "the Kelly".

The Kelly Bag

With a single handle and shoulder strap, the Kelly bag is both classy and practical.

All Kelly bags are exclusively handmade and can come with a waiting list of six years or more, and the bag is now available from mini-sizes right through to briefcases.

66

People were calling the magazine
and saying, 'What bag is that?' and
calling Hermès saying, 'I want the
bag Princess Grace is carrying.'

99

Caitlin Donovan

Head of Sales for Christie's Handbags & Accessories Department,
graceinfluential.com, 2024

We cannot do an ugly gadget, because we would be ashamed if we compared it to this.

Ménéhould de Bazelaire

Curator of the Hermès museum, on the intersection of history and innovation that makes timeless pieces like a Kelly bag possible, vanityfair.com, August 27, 2007

Today, the Kelly bag comes in various styles, colours and sizes.

From dainty handbag to travel tote, it remains as iconic as the star who gave it its name.

"

I believe that it is right to honour all those who create beautiful things and give satisfaction to those who see me wearing them.

"

Grace Kelly, Princess of Monaco

On her fashion influence, awakenthegreatnesswithin.com, November 15, 2023

Unlike today's celebrities, Grace Kelly re-wore her brown Hermès bag so often that it became battered and worn.

In 2010, Kelly's very own bag was included in a Victoria & Albert exhibition on the style icon.

66

Our life dictates a certain kind of wardrobe.

99

Grace Kelly, Princess of Monaco

On her high society life that fit the Hermès style,
awakenthegreatnesswithin.com, November 15, 2023

To me, it's the antithesis of an 'It' bag… The attention to detail is unlike any other. There's no stitch that's accidental, there's no colour they've produced that's questionable.

Caitlin Donovan

Head of Sales for Christie's Handbags & Accessories Department, graceinfluential.com, 2024

A red Kelly bag was pivotal for the 2003 movie *Le Divorce*, starring Kate Hudson and Naomi Watts.

At a pivotal moment in the film, the bag is thrown from the top of the Eiffel Tower.

CHAPTER
THREE

THE BIRTH OF THE BIRKIN

THE HERMÈS BIRKIN IS ARGUABLY THE MOST COVETED BAG IN THE WORLD, WITH THE WAITING LISTS AND RESALE VALUE TO PROVE IT.

SO, WHERE DID THE MOST EXCLUSIVE BAG IN THE WORLD COME FROM? AND IS IT POSSIBLE FOR MERE MORTALS TO OBTAIN?

66

It's not a bag, it's a Birkin.

Sex and the City, Season 4, Episode 11, wmagazine.com,
November 30, 2022

99

The origins of the Birkin bag can be traced back to its namesake, the Anglo-French actress and singer Jane Birkin.

The story of [the Birkin's] creation
has gone down in fashion
history.

Karen Homer

The Little Book of Hermès, Karen Homer, 2022

My look is a cocktail. I'm not as nicely turned out as the French, but I don't care like the English.

Jane Birkin

The namesake of the Hermès Birkin bag, on her unique style, hellomagazine.com, July 16, 2023

Born in London in 1946, Jane Birkin had a prolific career as an actress, mainly in French cinema.

An "It-Girl" of the 1960s and 1970s, she was known for her quirky and boyish, yet sexy, style.

"

My best friend cuts my hair with
kitchen scissors.

"

Jane Birkin

This laid-back approach to fashion was indicative of Jane's style,
standard.co.uk, July 17, 2023

In 1979, Birkin caused controversy by recording a duet with Serge Gainsbourg of his song "Je t'aime… moi non plus."

Due to its explicit lyrics, the song was banned on radio stations across Europe.

"

Her style has become ingrained in the DNA of the Parisienne – insouciant, dishevelled and organic. An attitude more than a formula to dressing.

"

Osman Ahmed

Fashion writer and editor, bloomsburyfashioncentral.com, 2024

A key part of Jane's *laissez-faire* style was her wicker basket, which she carried everywhere from the shops to nightclubs.

It was the same wicker bag that she carried on an Air France flight from Paris to London in 1983.

66

Hermès is all about the discreetly unavailable.

99

Christina Binkley

Editor-at-large of *Vogue* Business, voguebusiness.com, July 17, 2023

Attempting to stash the wicker basket in the overhead compartment, the contents fell out and on to Birkin and her fellow passenger – Jean-Louis Dumas, CEO of Hermès.

Dumas suggested to Jane that she needed a bag with pockets, sparking a conversation that would change the face of handbags forever.

A handbag that is bigger than the Kelly but smaller than Serge [Gainsbourg]'s suitcase.

Jane Birkin

Recalling the sketch she made on the back of an aeroplane sick bag for the original Birkin, bbc.com, July 16, 2023

Dumas took Birkin's sketch
and turned it into reality.

In 1984, the first Birkin bag
was launched.

The first Birkin was a 35 cm design with space for the milk bottles that Jane carried for her children.

It also had a spacious pocket for her personal items.

"

In 1981, Jane Birkin… was sitting next to Jean-Louis Dumas on a flight between Paris and London when he noticed her overstuffed straw bag. 'You should have one with pockets,' he told her. 'The day Hermès makes one with pockets, I will have that.' 'But I am Hermès,' he told her and soon ordered up a variation on the Kelly with a similar belt and lock closure. The Birkin debuted three years later and became an instant hit.

"

forbes.com, August 20, 2014

The Birkin was a sleeper hit, really taking off in the 1990s during the era of the "It-bag".

It was popularized by celebrities such as Paris Hilton and the Olsen twins.

"

If I was a bag, this would be me.

"

Paris Hilton

On her custom made Rose Tyrien Birkin bag covered in Swarovski crystals. The bag's value was an estimated US$65,000 when purchased in 2018, pagesix.com, August 13, 2021.

A Birkin bag is a very good rain hat; just put everything else in a plastic bag.

Jane Birkin

The namesake of the world's most coveted bag had a rather cavalier attitude about the purse, standard.co.uk, July 17, 2023

The Birkin and Kelly bags are created from meticulously cut tanned leather, sewn together with the patented saddle stitch devised by founder Theirry Hermès in the 1800s.

Any bags that do not meet the high standards of Hermès are destroyed.

It's impossible to be stylish without confidence.

Jane Birkin

standard.co.uk, July 17, 2023

A specially trained Hermès artisan takes a minimum of 18 hours to create one Birkin or Kelly bag (or up to 40 hours!).

The Paris workrooms only produce five or six bags a week, creating a huge amount of demand and scarcity for these exclusive pieces.

"

[The Birkin] opened Hermès
up to new markets and customers,
but it also changed the typical
Hermès client.

"

Jérôme Lalande

The antiques dealer on how the Birkin bag revolutionized
Hermès' image, bbc.com, July 16, 2023

In 2009, *The Guardian* estimated that Victoria Beckham owned over 100 Birkin bags.

It is estimated that this collection alone is worth over $2 million.

Our business is about creating desire. It can be fickle because desire is fickle, but we try to have creativity to suspend the momentum.

Axel Dumas

Hermès descendant and CEO, forbes.com, August 20, 2014

The Birkin bag is so exclusive that even the fashion-rich *Sex and the City* costume department couldn't get hold of one in season five, opting instead to use a dupe.

> **"**
>
> [I was] super pregnant. Look how big that bag is. I mean, that bag had one job to do and it did it very poorly. Maybe if it was a real Hermès bag, it would've done a better job.
>
> **"**

Sarah Jessica Parker

On using a fake Birkin to cover her baby bump in season five of *Sex and the City*, image.ie, March 18, 2022

In 2015, the catalyst for the Birkin bag, Jane Birkin herself, stated in a public letter that she no longer wanted to be associated with the item, due to concerns over the ethics of crocodile farming.

I have asked the Hermès Group to rename the Birkin until better practices responding to international norms can be implemented for the production of this bag.

Jane Birkin

Expresses concern over the use of crocodile farming to create the Birkin, independent.co.uk, July 29, 2015

However, Hermès assured Birkin that they were investigating the claims and the actress relinquished, and so today the Birkin is still named after its original muse.

"

So here is the irony. The most classic and iconic bag on the planet, but my fans don't relate to it because it represents something they don't have. So how do I create and make it into something that they will love and adore, and turn it into a performance-art piece in itself?

"

Lady Gaga

On customizing her Birkin with a message to fans, nypost.com, July 14, 2014

In 2022, the Himalaya Birkin broke the world record for most expensive bag.

Valued at over $450,000, the bag was crafted out of crocodile skin dyed in a grey and white variant and adorned with18-karat gold hardware with over 200 diamonds.

Talk about one of a kind!

Time is our greatest weapon.

Jean-Louis Dumas

Former Hermès CEO. With the resale value of a vintage Birkin bag now being twice that of a new one, it's safe to say that Dumas was right, vanityfair.com, August 27, 2007.

> 66
>
> The Birkin bag is arguably the most famous and coveted handbag on both the primary and secondary markets. 99

Anthony Barzilay Freund

harpersbazaar.com, June 14, 2024

I remember when I met Axel,
I said I really want to make the coat
as relevant as the Birkin bag, and
I think today we have customers
who really discover the brand
through the ready-to-wear, and
that's something which is quite
exciting.

Nadège Vanhée-Cybulski

Creative director of Hermès International, on meeting Axel Dumas
and being inspired by the Birkin, vogue.com, June 6, 2024

The biggest and most expensive collection of Hermès bags is said to be owned by Singaporean socialite, YouTuber and influencer Jamie Chua.

As of 2022, she claimed to have over 200 Hermès bags, many of these being top-end Birkins.

> **"**
>
> The resale value of… the Birkin
> and Kelly bags over the past 10 years
> has outpaced gold.
>
> **"**

James Firestein

Founder of luxury resale and authentication platform OpenLuxury,
fortune.com, March 27, 2024

The philosophy of Hermès is to keep craftsmanship alive.

Axel Dumas

Hermès descendant and CEO, forbes.com, August 20, 2014

Obtaining a Birkin bag is not a simple matter.

For one, there is a strict naming convention for Hermès bags: "Hermès, size, bag type, texture, colour".

For example: "Hermès 25 Birkin Bag Togo in black" would be a 25 cm wide Birkin, made from togo leather (a signature material for the brand) in the colour black.

66

We don't have a policy of image,
we have a policy of product.

99

Jean-Louis Dumas

vanityfair.com, Laura Jacobs, August 27, 2007

A Birkin don't make you.
Don't ever feel like you gotta
compare yourself.

Cardi B

The rapper offers words of wisdom to those of us who dream of
owning a Birkin bag, businessinsider.com, October 27, 2020

CHAPTER
FOUR

THE ART OF THE SCARF

THE HERMÈS SCARF IS YET ANOTHER EXAMPLE OF CENTURIES OF CRAFTSMANSHIP MEETING FASHION AT JUST THE RIGHT TIME.

SINCE ITS INCEPTION IN 1927, THE VERSATILE ART THAT IS THE HERMÈS SCARF HAS GRACED THE HEADS, NECKS AND SHOULDERS OF EVERYONE FROM GRACE KELLY TO STREETWISE FASHIONISTAS.

The Hermès silk carré (which simply translates as "square") is a symbol of timeless luxury and elegance.

I think people want to be more in style than in fashion.

Jean-Louis Dumas

nytimes.com, October 18, 1986

From the 1920s, Hermès sold scarves made by Bianchini-Ferier, a quality silk house, alongside their own products.

As their reputation for artistic excellence grew in the early 20th century, Robert Dumas commissioned an exclusive scarf design.

66

Every Hermès scarf has a tale.

99

Christina Binkley

Editor-at-large of *Vogue* Business, wsj.com, May 22, 2013

Working with artist Hugo Grygkar, Dumas created the first Hermès scarf in 1937.

The *Jeu des Omnibus et Dames Blanches* scene printed on the scarf, depicting fashionable card players, was inspired by a 1830s board game owned by Émile Hermès.

I had never had an Hermès scarf.
And I ran to buy one, thinking,
'Now, this is a symbol, I need one,
I need an Hermès scarf.'

Lou Doillon

French-British singer, actress and daughter of Jane Birkin,
quote.org

Types of Hermès Scarves

Classic
The classic square shape

Twilly
A long and narrow silhouette with diagonally hemmed ends

Triangle
An elongated three-pointed scarf

Losange
A lengthened rhombus

The small luxury of beautifully printed silk landed just before the Second World War.

Durable and beautiful, the scarves provided a bright spark to many in a world of conflict.

"

Every Hermès scarf is made from pure silk. They use only the most luxurious silk, created by Bombyx Mori silkworms housed in a special facility in Brazil.

"

dresscheshire.com, 2022

A good player never loses his temper.

The inscription on the first Hermès scarf,
Jeu des Omnibus et Dames Blanches by artist Hugo Grygkar,
released in 1937

Since 1937, Hermès has produced over 2,000 unique designs.

An Hermès scarf is sold somewhere in the world every 25 seconds.

Hugo Grygkar continued as Hermès' most prolific designer, creating silk scarves until his death in 1959.

Celebrity fans of the silk scarf during the 1950s and 1960s included Audrey Hepburn, Jackie O and Catherine Deneuve.

Silk is a beautiful object that I want to move into the future.

Cécile Pesce

The current creative director of Hermès women's silk, wallpaper.com, July 22, 2023

"

When I wear a silk scarf I never
feel so definitely like a woman, a
beautiful woman.

"

Audrey Hepburn

vogue.co.uk, June 14, 2021

Much like the Kelly bag, Princess of Monaco Grace Kelly is synonymous with the Hermès scarf.

From donning an Hermès headscarf on the silver screen, to using one as a makeshift arm sling, Kelly was ahead of her time in showing the versatility of the Hermès scarf.

To receive one's first Hermès scarf – it's not about coming up in the world but about embracing it.

Laura Jacobs

Vanity Fair editor, vanityfair.com, August 27, 2007

117

The Hermès carré
is part of a French tradition
where a girl is presented with
a silk scarf on her sixteenth
birthday to mark her passage
into adulthood.

" My first love. "

Robert Dumas

More introverted than his father-in-law who preceded him as head of Hermès, Dumas was an early ambassador of the silk scarf, vanityfair.com, August 27, 2007

By 1979, the Hermès scarf had fallen out of favour with the new generation of fashionistas.

To counteract this, in 1979, visionary Hermès CEO Jean-Louis commissioned a series of ground-breaking advertisements, featuring hip young Parisians dressed in jeans with Hermès scarves hanging out of their back pockets.

The young customers came to us more than we went to them. People saw again, but with a new eye, the beauty of materials worked by fine hands. They came. We followed.

Jean-Louis Dumas

In a 1986 *New York Times* interview, reflecting on the successful integration of the Hermès scarf into eighties fashion, nytimes.com, October 18, 1986

Contemporary Hermès carré scarves are woven from the silk of 250 mulberry moth cocoons.

Two collections are produced annually as well as re-releases of vintage designs and special editions.

[The colours] are mixed from memories. The idea is to reorganize everything; colours are like words to make a sentence. Or how it is to make music: it is natural for me.

Cécile Pesce

The current creative director of Hermès women's silk, wallpaper.com, July 22, 2023

75,000 shades in the
Hermès colour catalogue
are mixed and perfected into
their (secret) formulas.

Colour is a costume for a
Hermès scarf.

Bali Barret

Artistic director, Hermès silk department (2003–2020), *The Story of the Hermès Scarf*, Laia Farran Graves, 2023

A woman without a scarf is a woman without a future.

Elizabeth Taylor

liftthelyd.co.uk, August 2, 2020

In France, we get acquainted with Hermès at a very early age. Your mom always has a scarf; it's one of the first objects you look at as a child, and you know it's precious.

Nadège Vanhée-Cybulski

Creative director of Hermès International (2014–present), *The Story of the Hermès Scarf*, Laia Farran Graves, 2023

> **"**
>
> A scarf has to be the most beautiful thing ever invented to wear! It's a winding, a continuity and infinity! I love things that are endless, I hate them to stop.
>
> **"**

Sonia Rykiel

The Story of the Hermès Scarf, Laia Farran Graves, 2023

Today, many notable designers have collaborated on the creation of Hermès scarves, such as Alexander McQueen and Donatella Versace.

A big fan of the Hermès scarf, Queen Elizabeth II was the inspiration for a limited-edition design released in 2016, to celebrate her 90th birthday.

CHAPTER
FIVE

A READY-TO-WEAR REVOLUTION

NO FASHION HOUSE
WOULD BE COMPLETE WITHOUT
A READY-TO-WEAR LINE.

WITH ITS SIGNATURE
COMMITMENT TO DETAIL AND
STRATEGIC PARTNERSHIPS WITH
EXCITING DESIGNERS, HERMÈS
WOMENSWEAR IS THE ULTIMATE
DEFINITION OF CHIC.

At the beginning of the century,
a woman came in and said:
'I'm fed up seeing my horse better
dressed than me. When will you
dress ladies?'

Flavie Chaillet

The Hermès press representative speaking to the *New York Times*,
October 18, 1986

On the behest of this particular customer, Hermès began to produce clothing in the early 1910s.

By 1922, exquisitely made outfits were being sold along with watches and gloves.

"

Hermès offers a sense of refinement.

"

Dawn Mello

Former president of Bergdorf Goodman department stores, nytimes.com, October 18, 1986

In keeping with the Hermès tradition of supplying royalty, Edward, Prince of Wales was the first to sport an Hermès leather golf jacket in 1918.

Designed specifically for him, the jacket contained a zipper – cutting-edge technology patented by Hermès at the time.

I'm not a beautiful woman.
I'm nothing to look at, so the only
thing I can do is dress better than
anyone else.

Wallis Simpson

She and her husband, Edward the Duke of Windsor, were lifelong
fans of Hermès, ellecanada.com, September 19, 2011

"

When you flick through the archives, lots of women have given a strong imprint to the House, even though the first clothes designed for women were men's adaptations.

"

Nadège Vanhée-Cybulski

Creative director of Hermès International (2014–present) on the history of Hermès fashion, vogue.com, June 6, 2024

Hermès quickly introduced accessories and jewellery to complement their clothing lines from 1925–1927.

However, it was not until 1967, forty years later, that the luxury goods maker introduced its first women's ready-to-wear collection.

When Hermès craftspeople and designers retire, they join the Club des Anciens (The Ancients) and meet for monthly and yearly trips, serving as living wisdom for the next generation of workers!

66

The idea is always the same at Hermès, to make tradition live by shaking it up.

99

Jean-Louis Dumas

vanityfair.com, August 27, 2007

Catherine de Károlyi designed the first ready-to-wear collection for Hermès.

De Károlyi arrived in Paris in 1948 as a Hungarian refugee, self-taught seamstress, model and designer and ran her own label until she was approached by Hermès.

She was the first to define what has never ceased to constitute Hermès since, the idea of elegance in motion.

Ménéhould de Bazelaire

Director of cultural heritage at Hermès, on the legacy of Catherine de Károlyi, lemonde.fr, August 16, 2024

The letter H is symmetrical… it could make a buckle.

Catherine de Károlyi

On the creation of the legendary "H" Hermès belt buckle, leparisien.fr, March 10, 2015

H Belt Buckle

Used for belts and bags,
the H buckle was designed in
1967 by Catherine de Károlyi.

Sleek and stylish,
there have been countless
reinterpretations of this
unique fastening.

It was so successful that people lined up outside the Faubourg store. As a result of its popularity and for practical reasons, salesmen ended up naming it after the draw in which it was stored: the famous No. 5382 draw.

Hermès

hermes.com

However, the industry was changing and the demand for fashion made from natural materials was struggling to keep up with the introduction of synthetic materials throughout the 1960s and 1970s.

The House of Hermès began to stagnate.

Jean-Louis Dumas can be credited with turning the company's fortunes around.

He took over leadership of the House in 1978 and embraced youth culture as the future of Hermès.

I don't care if they're crazy,
I want talent!

Pierre-Alexis Dumas

Artistic director of Hermès, on the family motto when hiring
designers, *The Story of the Hermès Scarf*, Laia Farran Graves, 2023

It's the only stock in its sector to be in its eighth-straight year of double-digit growth.

Lehman Brothers Analyst

Discussing the ascension of Hermès at the turn of the millennium, vanityfair.com, August 27, 2007

[Hermès was for] a very, very, very old woman.

Éric Bergère

On the perception of Hermès clothing in the 1980s, nytimes.com, October 18, 1986

Éric Bergère was brought in by Jean-Louis Dumas in 1980 to modernize the ready-to-wear side of the business.

What had once been the pinnacle of style in the 1950s and 1960s had fallen out of favour with the next generation.

"

Before, Hermès was a faraway world. It was perfume, the square and maybe the bag your grandmother gave you… [Now it's a brand] every Parisian girl could die for.

"

Kitty Fresnel

A young consumer explaining the changing perception of Hermès in a 1986 *New York Times* article, nytimes.com, October 18, 1986

But this brand is full of paradoxes. It's been around for 170 years, and yet it's a very young brand, because its geographical expansion happened in the last 20 years.

Pierre-Alexis Dumas

vanityfair.com, August 27, 2007

In April 1997, Hermès shocked the fashion world again when it announced that iconoclastic designer Martin Margiela would take the role of creative director of womenswear.

On the surface, the pairing seemed unusual, but the creative tension between Margiela's deconstructionist approach and Hermès' commitment to quality proved to be a match made in fashion heaven.

Anybody who's aware of what life is in a contemporary world is influenced by Margiela.

Marc Jacobs

Margiela: The Hermès Years, Kaat Debo et al., 2021

"

These are not entirely divergent worlds… the overall vision of Martin, resisting the fashion system, resisting… in a very conceptual way. And at Hermès, it was this slowly evolving wardrobe… For me it is 'slow' fashion before the concept even existed.

"

Kaat Debo

Curator of the MoMu Fashion Museum in Antwerp, Belgium, vogue.it, March 30, 2017

While Margiela and Hermès both placed value in clothes lasting a lifetime, the Belgian designer took this concept one step further – with garments that could be worn multiple ways.

For example, coats that could be turned into capes with cleverly placed holes, sweatshirts that could be worn inside out and coats with interchangeable collars.

Margiela shunned the spotlight, often working alone and communicating only by fax.

His commitment to personal privacy is so strong that he is often referred to as the "Banksy" of couture.

I threw out a few names, but finally when I got home, I said to myself, 'Me. I would love to do it.' It's a house that allows for great creative freedom with no limits.

Jean Paul Gaultier

Recounting a meeting held with Jean-Louis Dumas that inspired him to take the reins of Hermès ready-to-wear, vanityfair.com, August 27, 2007

In 2003, Margiela left Hermès to focus on his own label.

In another shocking move, Hermès appointed the "bad boy of fashion" Jean Paul Gaultier to take over the womenswear creative director role.

The decision made sense commercially, as Hermès already owned a 35% stake in Gaultier's eponymous fashion house.

I've always admired, since I was a child, the luxury and tradition of Hermès… And Hermès' Caleche was my mother's favourite perfume.

Jean Paul Gaultier

nytimes.com, July 9, 1999

I believe that Gaultier has the ability to be what Hermès has become.

Jean Paul Gaultier

In a 1999 *New York Times* interview on Gaultier, the *enfant terrible* of fashion, nssmag.com, May 24, 2024

A love match rather than a business arrangement.

Jean-Louis Dumas

On the partnership between Jean Paul Gaultier and Hermès, nytimes.com, July 9, 1999

I learned, I respected the codes. It is a house with incredible know-how and technique. But I didn't betray who I was either.

Jean Paul Gaultier

On this time at Hermès, france24.com, October 9, 2010

Jean Paul Gaultier announced himself on to the Hermès stage with the Autumn/Winter 2004 collection, staged, fittingly, given Hermès' equestrian background, in the École Militaire cavalry training ground.

Gaultier wowed critics and clients alike, adding a sexy edginess to Hermès' traditional luxury fabrics, through clever tailoring and a rich colour palette.

"

[Hermès is] the world's greatest sex shop – with its whips, saddles, spurs.

"

Helmut Newton

Famously witty photographer, *The Little Book of Hermès*, Karen Homer, 2022

Gaultier stayed with Hermès until 2010, when he left to work on his own label. He was replaced by former head of Lacoste, Christophe Lemaire.

In contrast to Gaultier's flamboyant styles, Lemaire was far more similar to Margiela, with a focus on understated chic and elegant functionality.

At Hermès, we don't say we do luxury. We do useful objects of an extreme quality. You have to think about the comfort, the functionality, the pockets, the way the clothes will age. The inside is as important as the outside. The extreme quality that you feel, rather than show, is extremely important.

Christophe Lemaire

Perfectly summing up his four-year tenure at Hermès, qz.com, July 21, 2014

In 2014, Christophe Lemaire handed the womenswear reins to Nadège Vanhée-Cybulski, who remains artistic director of women's ready-to-wear to this day.

Jean Paul Gaultier had a lot of freedom at the House. He was really experimental, he tried to expand the scope of the silhouette while still playing with ideas like fetishism. Martin Margiela before Gaultier was a sort of chiropractor or osteopath. The House had gone in every direction and he really helped to consolidate the fundamentals.

Nadège Vanhée-Cybulski,

On her predecessors, vogue.com, June 6, 2024

As far as competitors, there are two
I admire: Chanel and Hermès.

Bernard Arnault

High praise from the main competition, billionaire head of French
luxury goods group LVMH, ft.com, July 8, 2013

CHAPTER
SIX

THE SIXTEEN MÉTIERS

MÉTIERS REFERS TO THE
SIXTEEN LINES THAT MAKE
UP HERMÈS.

FROM SCENTS TO MENSWEAR,
JEWELLERY AND HOMEWARE,
THIS IS A WHISTLE-STOP TOUR OF
THE REMAINING MÉTIERS.

Métiers

The sixteen lines that make up
the House of Hermès.

Each season the lines are designed
around a central "theme" that
ties them together, while giving
their respective creative directors
freedom to experiment.

The Hermès Métiers

Leather goods and equestrian

Women's silk

Men's silk

Women's ready-to-wear

Men's ready-to-wear

Shoes

Belts

Hats

Gloves

Jewellery

Watchmaking

Perfumes

Beauty

Furniture and Art de vivre

Tableware

Petit h

> **"** Jean-Louis Dumas said, 'Do what you want' and I thought, 'Oh, my God…' And I'm still doing it! **"**

Véronique Nichanian

gq-magazine.co.uk, March 20, 2019

Men's ready-to-wear

Unlike the majority of heritage fashion houses, Hermès' clothing roots lay in menswear. Since the first leather jacket in the 1910s, the House has continually re-defined men's fashion.

Véronique Nichanian has been head of Hermès menswear since 1988. After the death of Karl Lagerfeld, she is now the longest-serving non-founding designer at a Paris fashion house.

Like everybody, I have many lives.
I want clothes that are modern
and intelligent. So, I play a lot
on functionality to appeal to the
different lifestyles of the clients.
But I never lose the sensuality and
also the construction, the way
things are made.

Véronique Nichanian

In a 2019 GQ interview, gq-magazine.co.uk, March 20, 2019

Nichanian's tenure as head of menswear in Hermès has been undeniably successful, catered to those who like "beautiful things, beautifully done, in nice materials... with a sense of humour".

GQ, 2019

Some people like big diamonds –
for me, it's fabrics.

Véronique Nichanian

In a 2020 *Financial Times* interview, ft.com, March 13, 2020

While the Hermès Home Universe began with blankets and lamps, the House kicked it up a notch in 1924 with the appointment of interior decorator Jean-Michel Frank.

Using Hermès master saddlers, he designed pieces for the home using the core material of Hermès – leather: onseats, furniture and even walls.

Scents

Another central tenet of the Hermès universe is perfume.

The first Hermès eau de parfum for women, Calèche, was launched in 1951.

Nine years later, the first scent for men, Equipage, was released.

The *Hermès 24 Faubourg* perfume, a sunny, chic floral with hints of sweetness, was supposedly a favourite of Princess Diana.

The Best-Selling Hermès Fragrances (2024)

- Terre d'Hermès
- Un Jardin Sur Le Nil
- Twilly d'Hermès
- Jour d'Hermès
- Voyage d'Hermès
- H24 by Hermès
- Eau d'Orange Verte

Hermès employs an in-house "nose"; a specially trained perfumer responsible for establishing the scent profile of the house.

We push boundaries…
Everyone knows a Hermès piece is
honest and well done.

Charlotte Macaux Perelman

Artistic co-director of Hermès Home Universe,
homeanddecor.co.sg, January 16, 2018

Hermès Jewellery

One of the older métiers, Hermès has been designing jewellery since 1927.

Key pieces:

Collier de chien bracelet *(1927)*

Filet de selle bracelet *(1927)*

Chaîne d'ancre bracelet *(1951)*

The Hermès enamel bracelet *(1976)*

Hermès H "Clic Clac" *(1990)*

Watches

Émile Hermès designed the House's first wristwatch in 1912 as a gift to his daughter.

From 1928, the brand began taking watchmaking seriously, partnering with the Swiss watchmakers Movado.

Today, Hermès produces more than 60,000 watches a year.

The patented Hermès watch designs include: Médor, Kelly, Dressage, Arceau, Heure H, Slim, Galop, Cape Cod, Nantucket, Faubourg and Carré H.

They have also partnered with Apple to create a leather wrist strap for the Apple Watch.

We are an industrial company with 12 divisions, which designs, makes and retails its products. We aren't a holding company.

Jean-Louis Dumas

On the central tenant of Hermès – to make beautiful, high-quality items, vanityfair.com, August 27, 2007

From saddles to stars of stage and screen, and from artisans to aristocrats, there is no other brand quite like Hermès. To own a piece of Hermès is to own a piece of handcrafted history.

Classicism as a modern way
of seeing life.

Nadège Vanhée-Cybulski

On the Hermès philosophy, vogue.com, March 3, 2019